START TH

Start the day well

by

BERYL BYE

LUTTERWORTH PRESS
GUILDFORD and LONDON

First published 1970
Reprinted 1974

ISBN 0 7188 1696 X

Printed in Great Britain by
Latimer Trend & Company Ltd Plymouth

INTRODUCTION

VARIOUS food manufacturers recommend us to "start the day" with their particular product. Surely every Christian family should "start the day" with a portion of God's Word?

Small portions are more easily digested than large ones, especially by the younger members of the family.

Start the Day Well follows the same pattern as my previous book in this series, *Prayers at Breakfast*, and is designed so that the whole family can take part, one reading the verses, one contributing the thought, one praying the prayer, and one saying the grace. We find in our family that participation prevents boredom!

The readings have been planned with the *Revised Standard Version* in mind, but some families may prefer to use J. B. Phillips for the New Testament. At the end of the book will be found special readings for the weeks before Easter and Easter week (pages 53–57); for Whit Sunday (page 58); for two weeks before Christmas and Christmas week (pages 59–61); and for the last week of the year (page 62).

BERYL BYE

ACKNOWLEDGEMENTS

SOME of the graces used are taken from *First Graces*, illustrated by Tasha Tudor, and published by Lutterworth Press.

The author is grateful to the editor of *The Church of England Newspaper* for permission to use prayers and graces which appeared originally in his columns.

Grace for the Week:

Dear Heavenly Father, we give Thee humble thanks for these Thy precious gifts, taken from Thy bounty. Bless the kind hands that have prepared them for our needs, and grant us Thy peace. Amen.

Monday:

Reading: Mark 2: 15–17.

Thought: Do we limit our friendships?

Prayer: Dear Lord, Help us to welcome into our hearts and our homes those who have never had the privilege of knowing You as their friend. Amen.

Tuesday:

Reading: Mark 3: 1–4.

Thought: Do we do good on the Sabbath?

Prayer: Dear Lord Jesus, Help us to use our Sundays for worship and for rest and for doing good to others as You intended. Amen.

Wednesday:

Reading: Mark 3: 5–8.

Thought: Do our hard hearts make Jesus sad?

Prayer: Forgive us, Lord, for the hardness of our hearts that makes us deaf to Your Voice and blind to the needs of others. Amen.

Thursday:

Reading: Mark 3: 31–35.

Thought: Do we do God's will?

Prayer: Dear Lord Jesus, Help us to be worthy to be called Your brother, Your sister, or Your mother, because we know we are doing Your will. Amen.

Friday:

Reading: Ecclesiastes 3: 12–13.

Thought: Do we take joy in our work?

Prayer: Help us to take a real joy in our work, dear Lord, so that we may know the satisfaction of receiving Your reward. Amen.

Saturday:

Reading: Ecclesiastes 4: 9–12.

Thought: Two are better than one.

Prayer: Help us to pull together in our family, O God, so that we may have strength against evil. Amen.

Sunday:

Reading: Ecclesiastes 5: 1–3.

Thought: Do we talk too much?

Prayer: Dear Father God, We confess to You today that we talk too much and listen too little. Quieten us before You now, O Lord, and speak to our hearts. Amen.

Grace for the Week:

For daily bread, for all things good,
For life and health, for this our food,
For each good gift Thy grace imparts
We thank Thee, Lord, with humble hearts. Amen.

Monday:

Reading: Genesis 40: 1–3.

Thought: God's servants are found in strange places.

Prayer: O God, use us in the place that you have put us, however distasteful that place may be. Amen.

Tuesday:

Reading: Genesis 40: 4–6.

Thought: Do we notice other people's feelings?

Prayer: Lord, help us to notice if anyone we know is sad today, and give us patience to listen to their troubles. Amen.

Wednesday:

Reading: Genesis 40: 8–11.

Thought: Do we give God the credit for our talents?

Prayer: God, help us to use the gifts that You have given us to Your glory, and not to our own. Amen.

Thursday:

Reading: Genesis 40: 12–15.

Thought: Do we take undeserved punishment meekly?

Prayer: Lord Jesus, teach us to bear patiently undeserved punishment, even as You bore Your unfair trial and cruel death. Amen.

Friday:

Reading: Genesis 40: 16–19.

Thought: We should be wary of wanting to see into the future.

Prayer: O God, who has told us to live one day at a time and to live it unto You, help us today to walk worthily. Amen.

Saturday:

Reading: Genesis 40: 20–23.

Thought: Do we remember our promises?

Prayer: Remind us today, Lord, of any promises that we have made and help us to keep them. Amen.

Sunday:

Reading: Genesis 41: 1–4.

Thought: God's plans sometimes have strange beginnings.

Prayer: Almighty God, who brought blessing to Joseph's family out of a king's dream, teach us to take part in Your plans even though we may not fully understand them. Amen.

Grace for the Week:

We thank Thee heavenly Father for this food and drink. With it also feed our souls with the Living Bread. Amen.

Monday:

Reading: Genesis 41: 5–8.

Thought: Only God can quieten our worries.

Prayer: Teach us to turn to You, Lord, when we are worried or troubled about anything. Amen.

Tuesday:

Reading: Genesis 41: 9–12.

Thought: Do we remember our faults?

Prayer: Bring to our minds today, Lord, any tasks undone, letters unwritten, or visits unmade, and help us to find the time to do the things we have left undone. Amen.

Wednesday:

Reading: Genesis 41: 14–16.

Thought: "Not me . . . God. . . ."

Prayer, Remind us, O God, to give You the credit for the gifts which You have given to us. Amen.

Thursday:

Reading: Genesis 41: 25–28.

Thought: Do we take notice of God's warnings?

Prayer: O God, we find many warnings in Your Book. Give us the good sense to take notice of them. Amen.

Friday:

Reading: Genesis 41: 29–31.

Thought: When bad times come, do we forget the good?

Prayer: Dear Father, when lean times come to us, remind us of our past blessings, and teach us to accept all things as from Your Hand. Amen.

Saturday:

Reading: Genesis 41: 33–36.

Thought: Good organizers are needed in God's work.

Prayer: Almighty God, we know that You have given to each of us different gifts. We ask You to show us if our gift is that of organization and if so to use it in Your service. Amen.

Sunday:

Reading: Genesis: 41: 37–40.

Thought: Do people see God's spirit in us?

Prayer: O God, we confess how seldom people see Your Spirit working in our lives. Forgive us, and help us to show forth more fully Your love and Your wisdom. Amen.

Grace for the Week:

Our Father as our heads we bow
For our food we thank You now.
May we this day to Thee be true
In all we think or say or do. Amen.

Monday:

Reading: Genesis 41: 41–43.

Thought: Are we ready to take responsibility?

Prayer: If You show us a job we should do, dear Lord, give us the courage to do it. Amen.

Tuesday:

Reading: Genesis 41: 46–49.

Thought: Joseph did his job well—do we?

Prayer: Dear God, we know that today each of us will have a special job to do, at work, at school, or at home. Help us to do it well, and to do it as for You. Amen.

Wednesday:

Reading: Genesis 41: 53–55.

Thought: Do people come to us for help in the time of their need?

Prayer: Dear Lord Jesus, who left us the command to "feed your lambs," make us watchful of every need of those about us. Amen.

Thursday:

Reading: Genesis 41: 56–57.

Thought: "For the famine was severe. . . ."

Prayer: O God, thank You for giving us regular and plentiful food. May we, in turn, give to others, so that those who are hungry may be fed. Amen.

Friday:

Reading: Genesis 42: 1–4.

Thought: Do we obey our Father?

Prayer: Dear God, as Jacob's sons obeyed his voice, give us obedient hearts to do Your will. Amen.

Saturday:

Reading: Genesis 42: 5–7.

Thought: Do we talk roughly to our brother?

Prayer: Our Heavenly Father, we confess how often we speak roughly to one another. Teach us to treat each other with love and courtesy. Amen.

Sunday:

Reading: Genesis 42: 8–10.

Thought: Jesus knows us. Do we know Him?

Prayer: Lord Jesus Christ, we know that each one of us is loved and recognized by You. Help us to come to know You as our Saviour and Lord. Amen.

Grace for the Week:

We thank You Our Father for life, for love, for friends, for food, for good in the world and for opportunities to serve You by serving our fellow men. Amen.

Monday:

Reading: Genesis 42: 13–17.

Thought: Do our words always stand the test of truth?

Prayer: O God, help us to speak the truth always so that our tongues are kept from lying and deceit. Amen.

Tuesday

Reading: Genesis 42: 18–20.

Thought: Are we "God fearing" men?

Prayer: Dear God, may all that we do and think and say, show that we respect and honour You. Amen.

Wednesday:

Reading: Genesis 42: 21–22.

Thought: Does our conscience prick us?

Prayer: Dear Lord, keep our conscience tender so that we may be aware of wrongs that we have done to others. Amen.

Thursday:

Reading: Genesis 42: 23–24.

Thought: Do we cause grief to those who love us best?

Prayer: Forgive us, Lord, for hasty words and actions that cause our loved ones grief. Amen.

Friday:

Reading: Genesis 42: 25–28.

Thought: Does God get the blame for everything?

Prayer: Help us to understand Your loving nature more fully, dear Lord, so that we do not so easily lay to Your charge each trial and sorrow of our daily life. Amen.

Saturday:

Reading: Genesis 42: 29–34.

Thought: Do we tell everything to our heavenly Father?

Prayer: Teach us good Lord, to talk to You each day and tell You all about our troubles and difficulties. Amen.

Sunday:

Reading: Genesis 42: 35–38.

Thought: If we trust God we should not be dismayed.

Prayer: We confess, Lord, how often we fail to trust You fully, and are therefore dismayed. Teach us to have faith in You in everything. Amen.

Grace for the Week:

God, we thank You for this food, for rest and home and all things good; for wind and rain and sun above, but most of all for those we love. Amen.

(Philemon's slave Onesimus (meaning "useful") had run away. In Rome he met Paul and became a Christian. They both realized that he must return to his master and Paul sends him back with this letter.)

Monday:

Reading: Philemon 4–7.

Thought: Does our love refresh the hearts of our fellow Christians?

Prayer: Dear Lord Jesus, teach us how to love unselfishly, so that we may bring other people comfort and happiness and refresh their hearts. Amen.

Tuesday:

Reading: Philemon 8–12.

Thought: Are we useful?

Prayer: Show to us, O Lord, ways in which we may be useful in our home, in our church, in our job, and in Your service. Amen.

Wednesday:

Reading: Philemon 13–14.

Thought: Do we consult others?

Prayer: Gracious Lord, remind us to consider the wishes of other people so that we are not so ready to take the course of action which follows most closely our own desires. Amen.

Thursday:

Reading: Philemon 15–17.

Thought: A purpose in everything.

Prayer: Teach us, dear Lord, that there is a purpose in everything and make us content to leave our lives in Your hands. Amen.

Friday:

Reading: Philemon 18–20.

Thought: Are we prepared to right other people's wrongs?

Prayer: Lord Jesus, if we should have the chance to right someone else's wrongs, help us to do it with all our heart, in gratitude to You who took upon Yourself all our wrongdoing and made us right with God. Amen.

Saturday:

Reading: Philemon 21–22 and v. 25.

Thought: Do we do more than we are asked?

Prayer: Dear Lord Jesus, grant to us the true spirit of service so that we may work the extra hour, walk the extra mile, or give the extra money, and do all with joy in Your name. Amen.

Sunday:

Reading: Psalm 122: 1, 2 and 6–9.

Thought: Are we glad to go to God's house?

Prayer: Dear Father, we thank you that we have freedom to go to Your House on Your day, and pray for all those Christians in other lands who must worship in fear and secrecy. Amen.

Grace for the Week:

Hear our prayer, O Lord, we ask,
And help us in our daily task.
Bless food and friends, and all men, too,
And through Thy grace our strength renew. Amen.

Monday:

Reading: Ephesians 4: 1–3.

Thought: Do we "put up with one another" in love?

Prayer: Give us, dear God, gentle and quiet behaviour, and teach us to "put up with one another in love" when quarrels or bad feeling seek to spoil our home. Amen.

Tuesday:

Reading: Ephesians 4: 25–27.

Thought: Do we ever go to bed whilst we are still angry?

Prayer: Remind us each evening, O Lord, to seek forgiveness for unkind words and actions before we go to bed, so that we may be at peace with our family, our fellow men, and with You. Amen.

Wednesday:

Reading: Ephesians 4: 28–30.

Thought: Does evil talk come out of our mouths?

Prayer: Help us to keep our words pure and clean, O Lord, so that we do not grieve Your Holy Spirit by what we say. Amen.

Thursday:

Reading: Ephesians 4: 31–32.

Thought: Are we kind to one another?

Prayer: Teach us to be truly kind to one another, and to put away all angry feelings, forgiving others, even as You have forgiven us. Amen.

Friday:

Reading: Ephesians 5: 1–4.

Thought: Are we walking in love?

Prayer: Help us to walk in love, dear Lord, and to praise You with our lips and our lives. Amen.

Saturday:

Reading: Ephesians 5: 15–17.

Thought: Do we make the best use of our time?

Prayer: Show us how to live wisely, O God, making the very best use of all our time. Amen.

Sunday:

Reading: Ephesians 6: 1–4.

Thought: Do we obey this teaching?

Prayer: O Lord, help us to listen to the advice that is meant for us, and to obey it with our whole hearts. Amen.

Grace for the Week:

Dear Father in Heaven, we thank Thee for this food, and for every gift that comes from Thee. Amen.

Monday:

Reading: Ephesians 6: 5–8

Thought: Do we only work when under our "master's" eye?

Prayer: Help us to do all our work well today, Lord, whether there is anyone to watch us or not. Amen.

Tuesday:

Reading: Ephesians 6; 10–13.

Thought: Are we strong in the Lord?

Prayer: Dear God, give us the strength to stand firmly against all the temptations of the evil one. Amen.

Wednesday:

Reading: Ephesians 6: 14–16.

Thought: A missing piece of armour means a weak place.

Prayer: Give us Your complete armour, we pray You, so that we may safely and surely enter the fights against evil and deceit. Amen.

Thursday:

Reading: Ephesians 6: 17–20.

Thought: Are we fearful of saying what is right?

Prayer: Strengthen us, O Lord, so that we may speak what is right, without fear. Amen.

Friday:

Reading: Ephesians 6: 21–24.

Thought: Have we undying love for Our Lord?

Prayer: O God, give us undying love for You today, and may we show our love in all we do and say. Amen.

Saturday:

Reading: Jeremiah 1: 1, 4 and 5.

Thought: God has a special work for each one of us.

Prayer: O God, show us the special work that you have given us to do, so that we may know Your will for our lives. Amen.

Sunday:

Reading: Jeremiah 1: 6–8.

Thought: God provides the tools for the job.

Prayer: Dear God, give us the faith to believe that You will equip us for the work to which You have called us. Amen.

Grace for the Week:

For this and every bounteous meal
Which Thou dost freely give,
Help us deep gratitude to feel
And to Thy glory live. Amen.

Monday:

Reading: Jeremiah 1: 9–10.

Thought: Sometimes God has to destroy before He can build.

Prayer: Dear Father, show us today if there is anything that must be removed from our lives before we can be fully used by You. Amen.

Tuesday:

Reading: Jeremiah 1: 14–16.

Thought: Have we forsaken God?

Prayer: Keep us ever faithful to You, O God, so that our worship is sincere and true. Amen.

Wednesday:

Reading: Jeremiah 1: 17–19.

Thought: Christians must be prepared to fight.

Prayer: Help us today to fight the good fight of faith, O God, and give us Your promised victory. Amen.

Thursday:

Reading: Jeremiah 2: 1–3.

Thought: Faith cannot live on memories.

Prayer: Give us a new love, a new faith, and a new trust in You every day, Lord, so that our Christian lives grow ever stronger and more victorious. Amen.

Friday:

Reading: Jeremiah 2: 4–6.

Thought: Do we forget past blessings?

Prayer: Thank You, dear Lord, for all the blessings You have showered upon us in the past days, and may Your hand be upon us in the future. Amen.

Saturday:

Reading: Jeremiah 2: 7–9.

Thought: Do we go after things that are not profitable?

Prayer: Loving Heavenly Father, teach us to seek after things of lasting worth and value that nothing can destroy. Amen.

Sunday:

Reading: Jeremiah 2: 21–22.

Thought: Soap and soda cannot remove sin.

Prayer: Cleanse us from our sins, Lord, by the precious blood of the Lord Jesus shed for us at Calvary. Amen.

Grace for the Week:

For the rest of the night, the light of the day, for our food, our fellowship, and for all the good things of life, we give Thee thanks, O Lord. Amen.

Monday:

Reading: Jeremiah 5: 23–25.

Thought: Do we give worship to God who sends the rain?

Prayer: We thank You today, dear God, for Your ordering of the weather and the harvest crops so that we may be fed. Amen.

Tuesday:

Reading: Jeremiah 5: 26–28.

Thought: Do we look after the poor and orphaned?

Prayer: Show us a practical way in which we can help our poorer brothers, O Lord, and show our love for children without parents. Amen.

Wednesday

Reading: Jeremiah 7: 1–3.

Thought: Do we give ear to the Word of the Lord?

Prayer: Remind us of the words we have read today when we next enter the doors of a place of worship, dear God, so that we may "give ear" to Your Word. Amen.

Thursday

Reading: Jeremiah 7: 22–24.

Thought: Backwards or forwards?

Prayer: Help us to progress in our Christian lives, dear Lord, so that every day we draw nearer to You. Amen.

Friday:

Reading: Jeremiah 20: 1–3.

Thought: People often do not like to hear the truth.

Prayer: Give us the courage to listen to the truth about ourselves, O Lord, and help us to be gracious under honest criticism. Amen.

Saturday:

Reading: Jeremiah 21: 1–4.

Thought: Do we seek God only when we want His help?

Prayer: We confess, O Lord, that we often think most about You when we most need Your help. Forgive us and help us to live always with You at our side. Amen.

Sunday:

Reading: Jeremiah 21: 8–10.

Thought: God's warnings should be noted.

Prayer: Help us to treat with respect the warnings that You have given to us, O Lord, and to choose the way of Life. Amen.

Grace for the Week:

Dear Father in Heaven, our thanks now we bring
For food and for clothing and every good thing.
O give of Thy blessings to all who have need,
And teach us to love Thee in word and in deed. Amen.

Monday:

Reading: Genesis 43: 1–5.

Thought: Are we wary of disobeying?

Prayer: O God, You have shown us today how Joseph's brothers were wary of disobeying his orders. Make us careful to obey you. Amen.

Tuesday:

Reading: Genesis 43: 6–10.

Thought: Do we waste time in arguing?

Prayer: Loving Heavenly Father, we know we often waste a lot of time in unnecessary argument. Help us to talk less and to act more. Amen.

Wednesday:

Reading: Genesis 43: 11–14.

Thought: Are we strictly honest in our dealings?

Prayer: We know that we must always be strictly honest if we are to be a good witness for You, O Lord. Make us very conscious of this every time we are tempted to cheat in any way. Amen.

Thursday:

Reading: Genesis 43: 15–18.

Thought: Do we mistrust people?

Prayer: Dear Father, give us a simple trust in the actions of other people, and teach us to accept kindnesses in a thankful and gracious spirit. Amen.

Friday:

Reading: Genesis 43: 19–23.

Thought: Do we accept our wealth as a gift from God?

Prayer: Dear God, You have given to us, as a family, all we have of material possessions. Thank You for supplying us so liberally. Amen.

Saturday:

Reading: Genesis 43: 24–26.

Thought: Do we look to the comfort of our guests?

Prayer: Gracious God, help us to look to the comfort of other people when they stay in our home, so that they may give the credit to You, who are the Head of our house. Amen.

Sunday:

Reading: Genesis 43: 27–31.

Thought: Is love or self-pity the cause of our tears?

Prayer: Dear Father, teach us to control the tears of anger and self-pity, and fill our hearts with brotherly love. Amen.

Grace for the Week:

For the night's rest, the morning meal, the new day and all the blessings it may bring, we give Thee grateful thanks, our heavenly Father. Amen.

Monday:

Reading: Genesis 43: 32–34.

Thought: Do we share our bounty with others?

Prayer: Lord God, remind us to share the bounty of our table with those less fortunate than ourselves. Amen.

Tuesday:

Reading: Genesis 45: 1–3.

Thought: Do we keep our family affairs private?

Prayer: Dear God, help us to be loyal to each other, and to discuss privately with our family any differences we may have. Amen.

Wednesday:

Reading: Genesis 45: 4–7.

Thought: Are we able to see God's plans through our own misfortunes?

Prayer: Teach us, Lord, to have the wisdom of Joseph, who could see Your plans more clearly than his own misfortunes. Amen.

Thursday:

Reading: Genesis 45: 9–11.

Thought: Do we want others to share in our success?

Prayer: When success and promotion come to us, dear Lord, give us the desire to share its rewards with others. Amen.

Friday:

Reading: Genesis 45: 15–18.

Thought: Other people are always watching our actions.

Prayer: Remind us that other people notice our words and actions, and help us, Lord, to refrain from behaving unworthily. Amen.

Saturday:

Reading: Genesis 45: 24–28.

Thought: Are we faithless?

Prayer: Give us true faith and simple trust, O God, so that we do not continually need to ask for proof of Your words. Amen.

Sunday:

Reading: 2 Corinthians 1: 3–4.

Thought: Can we give comfort to others?

Prayer: Help us, dear Lord, to comfort those in trouble with the comfort that You give to us. Amen.

Grace for the Week:

Thank you, God, for this good day
And all that makes it fair;
Our home, our family, food and friends
And for Your loving care. Amen.

Monday:

Reading: 2 Corinthians 8: 1–2.

Thought: Is our giving joyful and selfless?

Prayer: Teach us the joy of giving freely and generously, O Lord, to those who are in need. Amen.

Tuesday:

Reading: 2 Corinthians 9: 6–7.

Thought: Does God take pleasure in our giving?

Prayer: Direct, O Lord, the purposes of our hearts and show us how, to whom, and what to give. Amen.

Wednesday

Reading: 2 Corinthians 9: 12–14.

Thought: Is our giving the cause of much praise to God?

Prayer: Let our light so shine before men that they may see our good works and glorify our Father which is in Heaven. Amen.

Thursday:

Reading: 2 Corinthians 10: 17–18.

Thought: What is our Lord's opinion of us?

Prayer: We confess, O Lord, we so often seek for the approval of men. Help us only to seek for Your high opinion. Amen.

Friday:

Reading: 2 Corinthians 13: 11–14.

Thought: Do we live at peace with one another?

Prayer: Help us to live at peace with one another, and give us the harmony of the Holy Spirit in our home. Amen.

Saturday:

Reading: Jeremiah 36: 4–7.

Thought: God's Word still makes men sorry for their sinfulness.

Prayer: Thank you, dear God, for Your written Word preserved for us by the obedience of Your servants throughout the ages. Help us to take note of its teaching about our sinfulness, and be really sorry. Amen.

Sunday:

Reading: Jeremiah 36: 8–10.

Thought: Would we go without our food in order to hear God's Word read?

Prayer: O God, teach us so to value Your Word that we would be prepared to go without our breakfast, if necessary, in order to hear it read. Amen.

Grace for the Week:

Our Father, we thank You for Your care through the night and for all the comforts and joys from Your Hand this morning. Bless this food to our use, and keep us faithful and humble in Your service. Amen.

Monday:

Reading: Jeremiah 36: 19–21.

Thought: God's Book is meant to be read.

Prayer: Help us to read Your Book every day, our Father, so that we may lead our lives in accordance with its instructions and warnings. Amen.

Tuesday:

Reading: Jeremiah 36: 22–24.

Thought: Many men have tried to destroy God's Word.

Prayer: We thank You today, dear God, for Your Everlasting Word, which you have never allowed to be destroyed throughout the ages. Amen.

Wednesday

Reading: Jeremiah 36: 25–26.

Thought: Do we speak in defence of God's Word?

Prayer: Give us courage to defend Your Word, O God, even if people will not listen to us. Amen.

Thursday:

Reading: Jeremiah 36: 27–28 and v. 32.

Thought: Do we memorize God's Word?

Prayer: Help us to learn by heart portions of Your Word, dear God, so that it can never be taken away from us. Amen.

Friday:

Reading: Jeremiah 37: 11–14.

Thought: God's servants are often called upon to suffer unjustly.

Prayer: We pray today, O Lord, for all those imprisoned unjustly, because they are loyal to Your cause and seek to serve You with all their hearts. Be with them wherever they may be, and give them an assurance of Your everlasting love. Amen.

Saturday:

Reading: Jeremiah 37: 15–17.

Thought: Do we tell the truth at all costs?

Prayer: Help us to be strictly truthful, O Lord, even when we know that by being so we shall be punished or become unpopular. Amen.

Sunday:

Reading: Jeremiah 37: 18–21.

Thought: Do we listen to a plea for help?

Prayer: We ask you, loving Father, to make us watchful and ready to aid those in distress, whenever it is within our power to do so. Amen.

Grace for the Week:

For life and love and home and food,
For all Thou givest for our good,
We thank Thee, Heavenly Father.
Amen.

Monday:

Reading: Jeremiah 38: 1–4.

Thought: God's warnings are for our well-being.

Prayer: Dear God, who has given us warnings for our well-being within Your Book, help us to take note, and not to ignore them. Amen.

Tuesday:

Reading: Jeremiah 38: 5–6.

Thought: Do we try to "shelve" our responsibilities?

Prayer: Almighty Father, give us courage to do what we know we should do, and to say what we know we should say, whatever the cost may be. Amen.

Wednesday:

Reading: Jeremiah 38: 7–10.

Thought: Do we act quickly in an emergency?

Prayer: Dear Lord, help us to act calmly and wisely and quickly in an emergency, so that we may be of real use to those in trouble. Amen.

Thursday:

Reading: Jeremiah 38: 11–13.

Thought: Even cast-off clothes can be used in God's work.

Prayer: O Lord, make us thoughtful and thrifty so that nothing is wasted and we are enabled to use everything in Your service. Amen.

Friday:

Reading: Jeremiah 38: 14–16.

Thought: Do people hesitate to give us good advice?

Prayer: Dear Lord, make us willing to listen to suggestions and good advice so that we may benefit from experience of others. Amen.

Saturday:

Reading: Jeremiah 38: 17–20.

Thought: Obey now the voice of the Lord . . . and it shall be well with you.

Prayer: Teach us, O Lord, that in obedience to Your voice lies our safety and well-being. Amen.

Sunday:

Reading: Jeremiah 39: 15–18.

Thought: Service brings its own reward.

Prayer: We thank you for the way You watch over those who serve You, and we praise You because we know that our lives are in Your hand. Amen.

Grace for the Week:

For hot, good, fresh and wholesome food accept, dear Lord, our gratitude. Amen.

Monday:

Reading: 2 Thessalonians 1: 3–4.

Thought: Is our love for each other increasing?

Prayer: Grant, dear Father, that our love for You and for each other may increase more and more, day by day. Amen.

Tuesday:

Reading: 2 Thessalonians 3: 6–9.

Thought: Do we set a good example?

Prayer: Help us, dear Lord, to live orderly lives, working hard, so that we may set a good example to those with whom we work and play. Amen.

Wednesday:

Reading: 2 Thessalonians 3: 10–12.

Thought: Are we over-interested in the business of others?

Prayer: Help us, loving Father, to work quietly and not to concern ourselves too much with the business of others. Amen.

Thursday:

Reading: 2 Thessalonians 3: 13–16.

Thought: Do we get tired of well-doing?

Prayer: Be with us, Lord Jesus, in our daily tasks, and encourage us so that we do not tire of well-doing, but seek to serve You with our whole heart. Amen.

Friday:

Reading: Titus 1: 4–6.

Thought: Are we fit to be in authority?

Prayer: Dear God, to some of us You give positions of authority, at work, at school, or at home. Make us worthy of the position in which we find ourselves. Amen.

Saturday:

Reading: Titus 1: 7–9.

Thought: Are we lovers of what is good?

Prayer: Help us, dear Lord, to love the things that are good and to turn away from things that are wrong and evil and impure. In Your Name we ask it. Amen.

Sunday:

Reading: Titus 2: 1–5.

Thought: Does our behaviour bring credit or discredit to God?

Prayer: Dear Lord, give us good sense, sound faith, and steadfast love, so that we bring credit to Your Holy Name. Amen.

Grace for the Week:

We offer You, O God, our love and thanks for all You are and all You do for Your people, and we ask that Your grace may attend us now as we eat and talk. Amen.

Monday:

Reading: Titus 2: 6–8.

Thought: Good behaviour is a good witness.

Prayer: Help us to remember, O Lord, that our very lives are a witness to You and that we are constantly being watched by those who are not on Your side. Amen.

Tuesday:

Reading: Titus 2: 9–10.

Thought: Are we strictly honest?

Prayer: Help us to be on our guard against taking anything that does not belong to us, so that our honesty does credit to God our Saviour. Amen.

Wednesday:

Reading: Titus 3: 1–3.

Thought: Are we quarrellers?

Prayer: We have to confess today, dear Lord, how often we fight for our own way and fail to give in to others. Forgive us and help us to be gentle in our behaviour to all men. Amen.

Thursday:

Reading: 1 Peter 1: 1–5.

Thought: Guided by the power of God.

Prayer: Keep us safely day by day, Lord, so that by Your power we may be cleansed from all our sins and one day live with You in Heaven. Amen.

Friday:

Reading: 1 Peter 1: 14–16.

Thought: Are we holy in every detail of our lives?

Prayer: Remind us today, Lord, of any detail of our lives that is not pleasing to You, and show us what we must do to change it. Amen.

Saturday:

Reading: 1 Peter 2: 11–12.

Thought: Have we any good works for others to see?

Prayer: Dear Heavenly Father, we know that what we do is more worthwhile than what we say. Show us this week some good work that we may do for Your glory. Amen.

Sunday:

Reading: 1 Peter 2: 18–20.

Thought: Do we take punishment quietly?

Prayer: Help us to take quietly the punishment for our wrongdoing, especially when we feel that it has been unjust or undeserved, so that we may follow in Your footsteps. Amen.

Grace for the Week:

Thank You, Lord, for all the gifts You give,
Accept our praise and teach us how to live. Amen.

Monday:

Reading: Exodus 1: 7–10 and 22.

Thought: Cruelty can stem from fear.

Prayer: Dear Father God, we think today of people in other lands whose fear and ignorance are driving them to cruelty. Uphold all those who suffer at their hands, we pray You. Amen.

Tuesday:

Reading: Exodus 2: 1–4.

Thought: Are we a united, loving family?

Prayer: Dear Heavenly Father, as we read today of a mother's fearless love and a sister's obedience and patience, remind us of the family love and loyalty that we owe to each other and to You. Amen.

Wednesday:

Reading: Exodus 2: 5–8.

Thought: Have we pity for needy children?

Prayer: Dear Lord, show us any needy children whom we may help by gifts of money, clothes, or friendship. Amen.

Thursday:

Reading: Exodus 2: 9–10.

Thought: God's plans are more wonderful than ours.

Prayer: Almighty God, we are reminded today that Your plans are wiser and more wonderful than we often realize. Teach us to seek Your blessing on all that we do. Amen.

Friday:

Reading: Exodus 2: 11–12 and 15.

Thought: Are we hasty in our actions?

Prayer: Dear Father, we confess we so often act in haste and without due thought. Forgive us, and help us to control our words and actions. Amen.

Saturday:

Reading: Exodus 2: 16–17.

Thought: Do we defend the weak?

Prayer: Help us, dear Lord, to assist the helpless and defend the weak so that those in trouble may know that they can turn to us for help. Amen.

Sunday:

Reading: Exodus 2: 18–20.

Thought: Do we show our gratitude?

Prayer: Dear Lord Jesus, remind us to thank graciously those who have helped us in any way, and make us quick to note their needs. Amen.

Grace for the Week:

Gracious God, as we gather around this table to partake of our daily bread, we bow our heads in thankfulness for blessings showered upon us and for all Your loving care. Amen.

Monday:

Reading: Exodus 2: 21–25.

Thought: God always hears a cry for help.

Prayer: Dear God, teach us to turn to You for help in times of trouble, and meet our needs, we pray You. Amen.

Tuesday:

Reading: Exodus 3: 1–4.

Thought: God does speak to us in the course of our daily duties.

Prayer: Dear God, speak to us today as we go about our normal everyday duties and make us responsive to Your voice. Amen.

Wednesday:

Reading: Exodus 3: 5–6.

Thought: Do we treat God with true respect?

Prayer: Almighty God, we confess that we sometimes forget how great You are when we come into Your presence. Give us today a new sense of wonder at Your glory and Your power. Amen.

Thursday:

Reading: Exodus 3: 7–9.

Thought: Our present land is not our permanent one.

Prayer: Dear Father God, remind us that we are pilgrims journeying through this life on our way home to you, and help us to keep our eyes fixed on our heavenly goal. Amen.

Friday:

Reading: Exodus 3: 10–12.

Thought: Do we question God's choice?

Prayer: Gracious Lord, You know how unworthy we often feel to be used by You. Remind us that when You are with us we can do anything. Amen.

Saturday:

Reading: Exodus 3: 13–15.

Thought: How often do we ask God for the right words?

Prayer: Dear Father God, when people question us about You, give us the right words to answer them, so that they may be assured that You are the living God. Amen.

Sunday:

Reading: Exodus 3: 19–21.

Thought: Do we need wonders to convince us?

Prayer: Dear Lord, give us ready and obedient hearts so that we do not need wonders and miracles to convince us of Your presence. Amen.

Grace for the Week:

For food and all Thy gifts of love,
We give Thee thanks and praise,
Look down, O Father, from above
And bless us all our days. Amen.

Monday:

Reading: Exodus 4: 1–5.

Thought: Faith in God is more important than confidence in ourselves.

Prayer: O Lord, we know that it does not matter if we lack confidence in ourselves as long as we have faith in You. Strengthen our faith and help our unbelief. Amen.

Tuesday:

Reading: Exodus 4: 6–9.

Thought: Some people need a lot of convincing.

Prayer: Dear Father God, we confess that we are sometimes tempted to ask You for signs and wonders to strengthen our faith. Make us content to obey You without question. Amen.

Wednesday:

Reading: Exodus 4: 10–12.

Thought: Are we always making excuses?

Prayer: O Lord, we know that You will only ask of us those deeds which You know we are able to perform. Remind us of this when we make excuses. Amen.

Thursday:

Reading: Exodus 4: 13–15.

Thought: False modesty is a sin.

Prayer: Dear God, teach us the difference between modesty and false modesty, for we know that while one is a virtue, the other is a sin. Amen.

Friday:

Reading: Exodus 4: 18–20.

Thought: Are we willing to release our loved ones for God's service?

Prayer: Dear Father God, if at some future time you should call one of our family to serve You in a special way, help us to send him or her out with willingness and joy. Amen.

Saturday:

Reading: Exodus 4: 27–28.

Thought: Are our family ties unchanging?

Prayer: Loving Father, we think today of those relations whom we have not seen for many months or years. Keep the ties between us loyal and loving and unchanged, even though distance parts us. Amen.

Sunday:

Reading: Exodus 4: 29–31.

Thought: Do we pass on God's message?

Prayer: Dear Lord Jesus, You have given to us Your message of forgiveness and love, and goodwill to all men. Help us to tell this message to those who have never heard it. Amen.

Grace for the Week:

God is great and God is good, and we thank Him for this food. By His hand must all be fed—Give us, Lord, our daily bread. Amen.

Monday:

Reading: Exodus 5: 1–2.

Thought: Do we acknowledge God's right to command us?

Prayer: Almighty God, we confess that we sometimes question Your right to command our lives. Forgive us, and teach us to walk in Your ways. Amen.

Tuesday:

Reading: Exodus 5: 5–9.

Thought: Can we be accused of laziness?

Prayer: Dear Lord, help us to examine ourselves today to see if we could justly be accused of laziness, at work, at home, or at school. Give us a mind to work and strength to perform our tasks. Amen.

Wednesday:

Reading: Exodus 5: 15–19.

Thought: God's people often have to endure unfair and unjust treatment.

Prayer: Dear Lord, we pray today for Your people in other lands who are suffering cruel and unjust treatment at the hands of wicked men. Be very near them today, Lord, and encourage them through our prayers. Amen.

Thursday:

Reading: Exodus 5: 20–23.

Thought: Do we take our worries to God?

Prayer: Lord, when we worry about the work we are doing, and when complaints are made against us, teach us to take all our troubles to You. Amen.

Friday:

Reading: Exodus 6: 1 and 5–7.

Thought: God knows we sometimes need reassurance.

Prayer: Dear Father God, we thank You for understanding that there are times when we need Your comfort and reassurance, and for giving us the knowledge that You have made us safe and free by taking the punishment for our sins. Amen.

Saturday:

Reading: Exodus 6: 9–11.

Thought: "They did not listen."

Prayer: Give us listening ears, O Lord, so that we may be attentive when You speak words of comfort and encouragement to us through Your servants. Amen.

Sunday:

Reading: Exodus 7: 1, 2, 6 and 7.

Thought: No one is too old to serve God.

Prayer: We thank You, Lord, that no one is too young or too old to be able to serve You in some way. Show us the tasks most suited to our age and help us to do them well. Amen.

Grace for the Week:

Heavenly Father, bless this food, to Thy Glory, and our good. Amen.

(Pharaoh was very reluctant to allow the Israelite people to leave Egypt, where they served him so usefully as slaves, but the Lord was not to be trifled with, and at last even the proud Pharaoh had to obey the Almighty God.)

Monday:

Reading: Exodus 13: 17–18.

Thought: Do we try and avoid trouble?

Prayer: Dear Lord, give us peacemaking spirits so that we seek to avoid unnecessary trouble, and travel the ways of peace. Amen.

Tuesday:

Reading: Exodus 13: 21–22.

Thought: "To lead them along the way."

Prayer: Be with us continually, O Lord, guiding our footsteps by day and night, so that we may continue to "go on" steadfastly in the Christian life. Amen.

Wednesday:

Reading: Exodus 14: 1–4.

Thought: Do we sometimes feel as if the wilderness has shut us in?

Prayer: Lord, we confess that there are times when we are depressed and discouraged and we feel as if we are shut in a wilderness. Please rescue us from ourselves and show Yourself as the Lord of our lives. Amen.

Thursday:

Reading: Exodus 14: 5–9.

Thought: Do we suffer from hardness of heart?

Prayer: Give us hearts that are ever open to the needs and sufferings of others, we beseech You, our Father, so that we do not become selfish and self-centred. Amen.

Friday:

Reading: Exodus 14: 10–12.

Thought: Do we choose bondage or freedom?

Prayer: O Lord Jesus Christ, we thank You for dying on the Cross to save us from the bondage of sin and enable us to serve You in perfect freedom. Amen.

Saturday:

Reading: Exodus 14: 13–16.

Thought: "You have only to be still."

Prayer: Dear God, teach us today the wisdom of remaining in stillness and leaving You to fight our battles for us. Amen.

Sunday:

Reading: Exodus 14: 19–22.

Thought: Have we got God behind us?

Prayer: Almighty God, help us to walk fearlessly and uprightly in our daily lives, knowing that we have You behind us in all we say and do. Amen.

Grace for the Week:

Come, Lord Jesus, be our Guest, and let Thy gifts to us be blessed. Amen.

Monday:

Reading: Exodus 14: 23–25.

Thought: "The Lord fights for them."

Prayer: O God our Father, give us such victory over wrong-doing and temptation, that other people may say, "The Lord fights for them!" Amen.

Tuesday:

Reading: Exodus 14: 26–28.

Thought: Evil must eventually be punished.

Prayer: We would think seriously this morning, Lord, of all the wrong things that we have done that deserve to be punished. We are really sorry and ask You to forgive us because of Your death upon the Cross. Amen.

Wednesday:

Reading: Exodus 14: 29–31.

Thought: Do we recognize the works of God?

Prayer: Dear Father God, help us to recognize the many times when You do wonderful works in our lives, and please strengthen our faith in You. Amen.

Thursday:

Reading: Exodus 15: 1–2.

Thought: The same God for father and son.

Prayer: Heavenly Father, we thank You for the love we have for You. Grant, we pray You, that our children may love and serve You, so that together we may give You praise and glory. Amen.

Friday:

Reading: Exodus 15: 23–26.

Thought: The bitter can be made sweet by God.

Prayer: Lord Jesus, we confess how often we are guilty of bitter words and selfish and unkind actions. Live within us, we pray You, so that the bitter in our lives may be made sweet. Amen.

Saturday:

Reading: Exodus 16: 1–3.

Thought: Some people are never satisfied!

Prayer: Help us, O God, to be contented in the place that You have put us, and teach us that You will guide us through the rough places as well as the smooth ones. Amen.

Sunday:

Reading: Exodus 16: 4–7.

Thought: "A day's portion every day."

Prayer: Wise and loving Father, we know that we need both food and spiritual food each day to keep us healthy in our bodies and our spirits. Remind us to digest a "day's portion" of your Holy Word each day. Amen.

Grace for the Week:

Thou openest Thy hand, O Lord,
The earth is filled with good.
Teach us with grateful hearts to take
From Thee our daily food. Amen.

Monday:

Reading: Exodus 16: 11–15.

Thought: "Give us this day our daily bread."

Prayer: Dear Father God, You send us food each day in full measure even as You fed Your people in the wilderness long ago. Thank You for supplying our needs so regularly and generously. Amen.

Tuesday:

Reading: Exodus 16: 16–20.

Thought: Greed has no place in God's plans.

Prayer: We are reminded today, O Lord, of Your wonderful provision for the feeding of man. Teach us to use only what we need, so that we may have the means to assist in the feeding of Your hungry people in other lands. Amen.

Wednesday:

Reading: Exodus 16: 22–24.

Thought: Sunday work should be kept to a minimum.

Prayer: Almighty God, we sometimes forget Your wise rules concerning the Sabbath day. Show us how we can best organize our daily tasks so that one day a week may be kept free from unnecessary work. Amen.

Thursday:

Reading: Exodus 16: 25–30.

Thought: God always makes it possible to obey Him.

Prayer: Dear Heavenly Father, we thank You for giving us laws that it is possible for us to obey. Give us the desire to please You so that we both learn and love to obey Your will. Amen.

Friday:

Reading: Exodus 16: 31–36.

Thought: Do we remember God's past gifts?

Prayer: Dear Lord Jesus, remind us today of all that You have done for us, and all the blessings You have given us, so that we may relate to those who come after us the wonderful story of Your care and provision. Amen.

Saturday:

Reading: Exodus 17: 1–4.

Thought: Have we left "sin" behind us?

Prayer: Help us, dear Heavenly Father, to leave behind us our sin and wrongdoing, and to set our faces towards a new life in which we shall be continually guided by You. Amen.

Sunday:

Reading: Exodus 17: 5–7.

Thought: Do we try to put God to the test?

Prayer: O Lord, You know that we are sometimes tempted to test You, seeking to prove if You are with us or not. Give us a stronger faith and a deeper trust, we pray You. Amen.

Grace for the Week:

We ask You, O Lord, to accept our thanks for this food and keep us through the hours of this day. For Christ's sake we ask it. Amen.

Monday:

Reading: Philippians 1: 1–6.

(It is suggested that these readings are taken from J. B. Phillips' translation.)

Thought: Are our prayers a real joy?

Prayer: Teach us, Lord Jesus, the joy of prayer so that we may be faithful in bringing our friends to You. Amen.

Tuesday:

Reading: Philippians 1: 7–9.

Thought: Love is God's greatest gift to man.

Prayer: We pray today, Lord, that we may have still more love towards each other and our fellow men. Amen.

Wednesday:

Reading: Philippians 1: 10–11.

Thought: Do we recognize the highest and the best?

Prayer: O Lord, teach us to look for the highest and the best things of life and grant that our lives are full of true goodness. Amen.

Thursday:

Reading: Philippians 1: 12–14.

Thought: Do others take fresh courage from our actions?

Prayer: O Lord, help us to conduct ourselves with courage and faith in times of difficulty, so that others may be encouraged by our witness. Amen.

Friday:

Reading: Philippians 1: 19–21.

Thought: Do we honour Christ by the way we live?

Prayer: Lord Jesus, grant that our lives may bring You honour, and help us never to be ashamed to confess that we are Your servants. Amen.

Saturday:

Reading: Philippians 1: 23–26.

Thought: Are we helping others to progress in the faith?

Prayer: Dear Father God, use us in some small way to help others to go forward in the Christian life and to stand by those who need our help. Amen.

Sunday:

Reading: Philippians 1: 27–28.

Thought: Is our everyday life worthy of the Gospel?

Prayer: Remind us, Lord, that we serve You most often in the ordinary everyday things of life, and help us to live each day worthily. Amen.

Grace for the Week:

Our Father, with gratitude in our hearts we humbly bow in Your presence. While so many in the world are hungry, make us truly thankful for this food. Amen.

Monday:

Reading: Psalm 34: 1 and 7–10.

Thought: By experience we will see that the Lord is good.

Prayer: We thank You today for the experience we have of Your goodness, and for the way You so bountifully supply our every need. Amen.

Tuesday:

Reading: Psalm 34: 11–14.

Thought: Do we keep our tongue from evil?

Prayer: Heavenly Father, guard our tongues from speaking evil and words of deceit and use our lips in Your service. Amen.

Wednesday:

Reading: Psalm 34: 15–19.

Thought: The Lord is near the broken-hearted.

Prayer: Loving Father, we pray especially today for those in great sorrow or distress. Give them the comfort of Your very real presence. Amen.

Thursday:

Reading: 3 John: 1–4.

Thought: Is it well with our souls?

Prayer: Dear Lord Jesus, grant that we may live lives of sincerity and truthfulness so that all may be well with our souls. Amen.

Friday:

Reading: 3 John: 5–7.

Thought: Can Christian people testify to our love?

Prayer: Gracious Lord, help us to look after fellow Christians who come our way, especially those whom we have never met before, so that they may see our love for You. Amen.

Saturday:

Reading: 3 John: 9–10.

Thought: Do we want to put ourselves first?

Prayer: Lord of all power and might, make us wary of the sin of self-importance and remind us continually that he who would be greatest must be servant of all. Amen.

Sunday:

Reading: 3 John: 11–14.

Thought: Are we God's men?

Prayer: Dear Heavenly Father, grant that we may be worthy to be called men and women and children of God, and help us to spend our lives in doing good. In Your Name we ask it. Amen.

Grace for the Week:

As once again our fast we break,
Accept our thanks for Jesus' sake.
Amen.

Monday:

Reading: Acts 15: 22–26.

(It is suggested that these readings are taken from J. B. Phillips' translation.)

Thought: "Unanimously agreed."

Prayer: Help us, dear Lord, to discuss the work of our Church with other Christians and to reach full agreement before we put our plans into action. Amen.

Tuesday:

Reading: Acts 15: 30–35.

Thought: Do our letters bring encouragement?

Prayer: Dear Lord Jesus, we sometimes forget that our letters can be a way of bringing help and encouragement to other people. Guide our thoughts and our pens, we pray You. Amen.

Wednesday:

Reading: Acts 15: 36–40.

Thought: Do we argue over God's work?

Prayer: Heavenly Father, give us the gracious Spirit of the Lord Jesus within us so that we can work with other people in peace and love. Amen.

Thursday:

Reading: Acts 16: 6–10.

Thought: Do we respond quickly to a cry for help?

Prayer: Give us a true concern, dear Lord, for those who have never heard the good news about You, and make us ready to respond to appeals for our help. Amen.

Friday:

Reading: Acts 16: 11–15.

Thought: Has God "opened our hearts"?

Prayer: Dear Father God, open our hearts to the voice of Your Holy Spirit when He speaks to us, so that we may attend to His message. Amen.

Saturday:

Reading: Acts 16: 16–18.

Thought: The future is God's to reveal.

Prayer: Dear Lord, teach us the wisdom of leaving the future in Your almighty hands and help us to be content to know Your will for us one day at a time. Amen.

Sunday:

Reading: Acts 16: 19–22.

Thought: Are we false witnesses?

Prayer: Almighty God, please teach us to be honest and truthful when speaking about others, so that what we say may be a true account. Amen.

Grace for the Week:

Let us with a gladsome mind,
Praise the Lord for He is kind,
All things living He doth feed,
His full hand supplies our need.
Amen.

Monday:

Reading: Acts 16: 23–25.

(It is suggested that these readings are taken from J. B. Phillips' translation.)

Thought: Are we able to sing when in trouble?

Prayer: Dear Lord Jesus, give us the courage to sing in the midst of trouble, help us to be brave in the face of danger, and give us Your peace when we are faced with worries. Amen.

Tuesday:

Reading: Acts 16: 26–28.

Thought: Do we jump to conclusions?

Prayer: Dear Father God, You know that sometimes we imagine things that are not true and make up our minds without being sure of our facts. Teach us to pray before we act, at all times and in all circumstances. Amen.

Wednesday:

Reading: Acts 16: 29–34.

Thought: Do we know the way of salvation?

Prayer: O Lord Jesus, teach us the way of salvation from Your Holy Word, so that we may be sure of it ourselves, and be able to show it to others. Amen.

Thursday:

Reading: Acts 16: 35–37.

Thought: Public wrongs sometimes need to be publicly righted.

Prayer: Grant, O God, that the law of our land will remain fair and uncorrupted, so that nothing is done in a secret or underhand way. Amen.

Friday:

Reading: Acts 16: 38–40.

Thought: Are we in need of comfort, or can we give it to others?

Prayer: We thank You, Father God, for the men and women and boys and girls who serve You so faithfully that in the midst of their own trouble they are able to give comfort to others. Amen.

Saturday:

Reading: Acts 17: 10–12.

Thought: Do we read our Bibles regularly?

Prayer: Dear Father, give us a love and a hunger for Your Holy Word so that we learn to read and search it daily to discover Your will for our lives. Amen.

Sunday:

Reading: Acts 17: 16–18.

Thought: Open-air speakers must be prepared for mockery.

Prayer: We pray today, O Lord, for those who will be speaking of You in the open air. Give them wisdom to choose their words rightly, and courage to reply calmly to any who mock. Amen.

Grace for the Week:

Thine are the gifts, O God,
Thine our daily bread,
Let the naked feet be shod
And the starving fed. Amen.

Monday:

Reading: Acts 17: 19–21.

(It is suggested that these readings are taken from J. B. Phillips' translation.)

Thought: Are we carried away by new ideas?

Prayer: Dear Father God, help us to have a constant faith in You so that we may be contented to have You as our unchanging Saviour and Lord. Amen.

Tuesday:

Reading: Acts 17: 22–23.

Thought: Do we really "know" God?

Prayer: Almighty God, grant that our knowledge of You may increase day by day so that we know You and Your will for our lives. Amen.

Wednesday:

Reading: Acts 17: 30–34.

Thought: Do we "put off" our decisions?

Prayer: Dear Lord, You know how often we "put off" making decisions or doing tasks. Help us to decide wisely and to act promptly. Amen.

Thursday:

Reading: Acts 18: 1–4.

Thought: Do we help in the homes where we stay?

Prayer: Loving Lord Jesus, make us good witnesses for You in the homes where we visit and stay, so that we lend a hand cheerfully with whatever jobs may have to be done. Amen.

Friday:

Reading: Acts 18: 5–6.

Thought: Do we refuse to listen to God's message?

Prayer: Dear God, You know that sometimes we refuse to listen when You speak to us and prefer to go our own way. Keep striving with our stubborn hearts, we pray You, until we learn and love to obey. Amen.

Saturday:

Reading: Acts 18: 7–11.

Thought: "Let no one silence you."

Prayer: Dear Father God, give us courage to speak about You when we have the chance, at school, in the office, or amongst our friends. Amen.

Sunday:

Reading: Acts 18: 12–16.

Thought: Are we tale-bearers?

Prayer: O Lord, we find it so easy to criticize the words and doings of others and so easy to excuse our own ways. Help us to be silent when we are tempted to speak ill of others. Amen.

Grace for the Week:

Giver of life divine,
Who hast our table spread,
Preserve the lives Thyself hast given,
Feed us and make us fit for heaven.
Amen.

Monday:

Reading: Acts 18: 18–21.

(It is suggested that these readings are taken from J. B. Phillips' translation.)

Thought: "If it is God's will."

Prayer: Teach us, good Lord, to bring all our plans to You so that we know if it is Your will that we go forward. Amen.

Tuesday:

Reading: Acts 18: 22–23.

Thought: Do we put new heart into all the disciples?

Prayer: Use all of us, dear Lord, to encourage and strengthen those of Your disciples who have just started to follow You, and grant that nothing we say or do may hinder their progress. Amen.

Wednesday:

Reading: Acts 18: 24–28.

Thought: Do we make welcome new Christians?

Prayer: Father God, You have given us a happy and comfortable home. Show us ways in which we can use it for You and lead us to someone whom we can make welcome in it. Amen.

Thursday:

Reading: Acts 19: 8–10.

Thought: Do we speak with confidence?

Prayer: Dear God, You know that often we do not know exactly what to say when we speak about You to others. Give us boldness and confidence, we pray You. Amen.

Friday:

Reading: Acts 20: 7–12.

Thought: Do long sermons make us sleepy?

Prayer: O Lord, help us to be wide awake when Your Word is being preached, in case there is a message for us in the sermon. Amen.

Saturday:

Reading: Acts 20: 17–19, 22–23.

Thought: Would we face imprisonment and persecution for Jesus?

Prayer: Almighty God, we ask that You will be specially near those of Your disciples who are being ill-treated or imprisoned for their faith, and give us the same brave spirit that You give to them. Amen.

Sunday:

Reading: Acts 20: 33–38.

Thought: Giving is a happier thing than receiving.

Prayer: Dear Lord, please bring to our notice the needs of those less fortunate than we are, and give us the joy of giving to them of our plenty. Amen.

Grace for the Week:

We thank you, Lord, for this good food. Be with us as we eat it, and stay with each one of us throughout the coming day. In Your Name we ask it. Amen.

Monday:

Reading: Joshua 1: 10–11.

Thought: Do we prepare ourselves for service?

Prayer: Father God, teach us to prepare ourselves for Your service by every means within our power, and especially teach us to pray for Your help and guidance. Amen.

Tuesday:

Reading: Joshua 1: 12–15.

Thought: Do we help our brothers?

Prayer: Kindle in our hearts, dear Lord, a deep love for our fellow-men so that their fight may be our fight, their cause our cause, and their troubles our true concern. Amen.

Wednesday:

Reading: Joshua 1: 16–18.

Thought: Are we prepared to obey orders?

Prayer: Heavenly Father, train us to be worthy Christian soldiers, obeying orders and going wherever You would send us. Amen.

Thursday:

Reading: Joshua 2: 1–3.

Thought: Some of God's work has to be done secretly.

Prayer: Fit us, Lord, for the secret and silent jobs that mean little glory or reward but need a still tongue and a wise head. Amen.

Friday:

Reading: Joshua 2: 4–6.

Thought: What risks would *we* take to protect God's servants?

Prayer: Make us brave and courageous in Your service, Lord, bold in word and deed to encourage and protect those who also labour for You. Amen.

Saturday:

Reading: Joshua 2: 7–10.

Thought: God's care for us is a good advertisement.

Prayer: Dear God, help us to remember the many times when You have cared for us in a miraculous and wonderful way and give us the chance to tell others of Your provision for us. Amen.

Sunday:

Reading: Joshua 2: 11–14.

Thought: Do we keep faith with unbelievers?

Prayer: O Lord, grant us the grace to deal faithfully and truthfully with those who do not know You so that we do not bring doubt or discredit upon Your Name. Amen.

Grace for the Week:

For healthy appetites, and the means to satisfy them, we thank you, Lord. Amen.

Monday:

Reading: Joshua 2: 15–16.

Thought: Do we use our "wits" in God's service?

Prayer: Please put into our minds new and original ideas, O Lord, that through new means we may help to rescue people from the power of the enemy. Amen.

Tuesday:

Reading: Joshua 2: 17–20.

Thought: Are all those in our house safe from the enemy's attack?

Prayer: We pray today, Lord, for all within these walls. Guard and defend us, we beseech You, from the sinfulness and wrongdoing which so easily beset us. Amen.

Wednesday:

Reading: Joshua 2: 21–24.

Thought: Are we sure of final victory?

Prayer: Dear Father God, You know that there are times when we despair of conquering our particular sins and shortcomings. Remind us that we shall win in the end because of Your Victory on the Cross for our wrongdoing. Amen.

Thursday:

Reading: Joshua 3: 1–4.

Thought: Do we see the way we have to go?

Prayer: Show us more clearly, dear Lord, the path that You have planned for us to walk in, so that we may know the way we have to go. Amen.

Friday:

Reading: Joshua 3: 5–8.

Thought: God's greatest miracles need holy instruments.

Prayer: We remember, Lord, all the wrong things that we have done as we wait quietly before you now. Forgive us and cleanse us from all our sins so that we may be useful in Your service. Amen.

Saturday:

Reading: Joshua 3: 9–13.

Thought: Do we remember that we have a *living* God?

Prayer: Remind us afresh, Lord, that we do not worship a dead Lord but a living Saviour who is able to share in everything we say and do. Amen.

Sunday:

Reading: Joshua 3: 14–17.

Thought: It is necessary for leaders to stand firm.

Prayer: We pray today, O God, for the leaders of our church (especially . . .). We know that it cannot always be easy for them to stand firmly when they are busy and troubled. Give them the inner strength and peace that they need. Amen.

Grace for the Week:

For sleep to refresh us,
For a family to love us,
And for food to satisfy our hunger,
We thank You Lord. Amen.

Monday:

Reading: Joshua 4: 4–7.

Thought: One man — one stone.

Prayer: We bring before You today, Lord, the work of our Church. Show each member the job that you would have them do, so that the tasks are equally divided and no one is overburdened. Amen.

Tuesday:

Reading: Joshua 4: 8–11.

Thought: Do we see jobs through to the end?

Prayer: O gracious God, we confess how easy we find it is to start a job and how very hard sometimes to see it through to the end. Remind us of unfinished tasks and give us the staying power to complete them. Amen.

Wednesday:

Reading: Joshua 4: 14–18.

Thought: Leaders are only great when they are in close touch with God.

Prayer: Loving Lord Jesus, we sometimes forget that true greatness is not gained by our own effort but is a gift from You. Keep us in close touch with You so that we may strive not for our own glory, but for Yours. Amen.

Thursday:

Reading: Joshua 4: 19–24.

Thought: How often are our children told Bible stories?

Prayer: Dear Father God, give us, as a family, a love for Your Word and may we read and re-read the stories within it with increasing love and wonder. Amen.

Friday:

Reading: Joshua 5: 10–12.

Thought: God doesn't supply "manna" when "bread" is available.

Prayer: We pray today for those who will be fed or healed by the care and skill of ordinary means and human hands. Teach us not to expect miracles, when our needs can be met without them. Amen.

Saturday:

Reading: Joshua 5: 13–15.

Thought: Captains expect to be given leadership!

Prayer: Our Heavenly Leader, help us to hand over the management of our lives and plans into Your Hands as willingly and thankfully as your servant Joshua did so long ago. Amen.

Sunday:

Reading: Joshua 6: 1–5.

Thought: Do we go straight forward?

Prayer: Grant, dear Lord, that in our Christian lives we may go straight forward, and that You will save us from standing still or going backwards, or straying to the right hand or left. Amen.

Grace for the Week:

Heavenly Father, kind and good,
Who dost give Thy children food,
Accept the thanks we gladly bring—
Thanks to God for everything.
Amen.

Monday:

Reading: Joshua 6: 9–11.

Thought: Do we know the value of silence?

Prayer: Dear God, we know that each one of us needs to learn the value of silence. Help us to remain quiet when we are over-eager to defend or assert ourselves, and give us the grace to control quarrelsome, unkind and unnecessary words. Amen.

Tuesday:

Readings: Joshua 6: 12–14.

Thought: Getting up early is a good habit!

Prayer: Dear Father God, train us to rise early each morning to start the day with You, so that Your Presence and guidance go with us through the busiest day. Amen.

Wednesday:

Reading: Joshua 6: 15–17.

Thought: Perseverance is a necessary part of God's plans.

Prayer: Heavenly Father, You know how often we fail in our prayers and fail to overcome a besetting sin because we give up the fight too easily. Teach us that only those who persevere obtain the victory. Amen.

Thursday:

Reading: Joshua 6: 22–23 and v. 27.

Thought: Promises should always be kept.

Prayer: Make us careful to keep our promises, O Lord, both to fellow-Christians and to those who do not know You, so that we may be known as people who can be trusted. Amen.

Friday:

Reading: Joshua 23: 1–5.

Thought: "The Lord has fought for you."

Prayer: Dear Lord, grant that the only battles we fight may be the ones in which we can claim Your leadership. Amen.

Saturday:

Reading: Joshua 23: 6–9.

Thought: Do we obey the Bible?

Prayer: Thank you, Lord God, for Your Holy Word which you have given us as a guide-book. Help us to be strong to keep and do whatever it commands. Amen.

Sunday:

Reading: Joshua 23: 10–13.

Thought: Do we keep watch on ourselves?

Prayer: Heavenly Father, we confess we are always ready to keep watch over other people but less ready to keep watch on ourselves. Make us conscious of our faults and shortcomings so that we may continue in our love for You. Amen.

Grace for the Week:

Lord bless this food which now we take, and make us strong for Jesus' sake. Amen.

Monday:

Reading: Joshua 23: 14–16.

Thought: Christians can face death calmly.

Prayer: We thank You, Lord Jesus, for rising from the dead so that we can know that death is only the gate to everlasting life. Amen.

Tuesday:

Reading: Joshua 24: 14–15.

Thought: Whose servants will you be?

Prayer: We dedicate ourselves to You as a family this morning, O Lord, and pledge ourselves to be Your servants if you will give us Your help and strength. Amen.

Wednesday:

Reading: Joshua 24: 16–18.

Thought: "Never will we give up the Lord."

Prayer: Lord, you know there may be times in our lives when we are tempted to give You up for other things. Be very near us in our temptation and keep us faithful, we pray You. Amen.

Thursday:

Reading: Joshua 24: 19–21.

Thought: Only forgiven sinners can be true servants of God.

Prayer: Dear Father God, we know that our sin makes a barrier betwen You and us and prevents us serving You fully. Please take away whatever is wrong in our lives. Amen.

Friday:

Reading: Joshua 24: 22–24.

Thought: Do we give ear to God's voice?

Prayer: Speak through Your Word, speak through our minds and hearts, speak through the circumstances of this day, Lord, and grant that our ears may be in tune to hear Your voice. Amen.

Saturday:

Reading: Joshua 24: 25–28.

Thought: We have witnesses when we are false to God.

Prayer: Loving Heavenly Father, forgive us the times when we are bad and false witnesses to our faith in You and remind us that our lapses do not go unnoticed by others. Amen.

Sunday:

Reading: Joshua, 24: 29–31.

Thought: "True to the Lord."

Prayer: Keep each one of us true to the Lord throughout all our days, dear God, always praising Him for what He has done for us. Amen.

Grace for the Week:

God bless our meal
God guide our ways,
God give us grace,
Our Lord to please.
Amen.

Monday:

Reading: 2 Peter 1: 1–4.

Thought: Do we consider our faith 'valuable'?

Prayer: Almighty God, we pray today for those countries where people are not free to worship You openly and in freedom. Help us to value our faith more and to count it precious. Amen.

Tuesday:

Reading: 2 Peter 1: 5–7.

Thought: Does our faith carry with it goodness of life?

Prayer: Dear Lord, we find it very easy to call ourselves Christians, but it is very much harder to live a really good life. Give us Your Holy Spirit, we pray You, so that we become more like You. Amen.

Wednesday:

Reading: 2 Peter 1: 8–9.

Thought: Are we shortsighted?

Prayer: Give us honest and piercing inward sight, O God, which shows us where we fail and reminds us that we were cleansed from our former sins in order to be Your disciples. Amen.

Thursday:

Reading: 2 Peter 1: 10–12.

Thought: Are we zealous Christians?

Prayer: Give us energy and purpose as we work for You, O Lord, so that we do not fall into the sin of laziness and become Christians in name but not in deed. Amen.

Friday:

Reading: 2 Peter 1: 13–15.

Thought: Remind and recall.

Prayer: We thank You, dear God, for our older and wiser Christian friends who have so often reminded us of our high calling and whose advice we so often recall. Amen.

Saturday:

Reading: 2 Peter 1: 16–19.

Thought: Do we give close attention to God?

Prayer: Dear Father God, we often listen to Your Word with half our minds and half our ears. Help us to pay full attention when it is being read, so that it may be like a light shining where we need it most. Amen.

Sunday:

Reading: 2 Peter 1: 20–21 and 2: 1–3.

Thought: Are we wary of false prophets?

Prayer: Teach us to be wary of any teaching that disagrees with what we read in Your Holy Word, and hear our prayer today for all those who through ignorance declare false words to others about You. Amen.

Grace for the Week:

For health and strength and daily food we praise Thy name, O Lord. Amen.

Monday:

Reading: 2 Peter 3: 1–2.

Thought: Both the Old and New Testament are for our learning.

Prayer: Holy Spirit of God, plant in our hearts the words of the Holy Scriptures so that we may remember them in times of doubt or need. Amen.

Tuesday:

Reading: 2 Peter 3: 3–7.

Thought: Do we sometimes get tired of waiting?

Prayer: Lord Jesus Christ, keep us watching and alert so that we may see in the world the signs of Your coming again, and grant that we may serve You well in the time of waiting. Amen.

Wednesday:

Reading: 2 Peter 3: 8–10.

Thought: Do we try to keep God to our time?

Prayer: Dear Father God, help us to be patient towards others as You are towards us, remembering that in Your own good time our prayers for them will be answered. Amen.

Thursday:

Reading: 2 Peter 3: 11–13.

Thought: Are we people of good and holy character?

Prayer: Grant, O Heavenly Father, that by our good and holy lives we may show that we are expecting and hoping for You to come again. Amen.

Friday:

Reading: 2 Peter 3: 14–16.

Thought: Are we sometimes guilty of trying to "twist" the Scriptures?

Prayer: Dear Father God, forgive us if we sometimes try to "twist" Your Word, in order to make it suit ourselves. Grant us Your Holy Spirit's help so that all things may be made plain and clear. Amen.

Saturday:

Reading: 2 Peter 3: 17–18.

Thought: Are we growing in grace?

Prayer: As our knowledge of You grows each day, dear Lord, so help us to grow in grace also. Amen.

Sunday:

Reading: John 6: 1–6.

Thought: Jesus always knows how to solve our difficulties.

Prayer: Lord Jesus, You know that there are times when we have a special problem to solve and do not know what to do about it. Remind us that You know the answer even if we do not. Amen.

Grace for the Week:

May we who have plenty,
Remember those who have not,
And may we waste nothing that is good to eat,
And comes from Thy Hand, O God. Amen.

Monday:

Reading: John 6: 7–12.

Thought: Jesus doesn't like waste.

Prayer: Loving Lord Jesus, help us to use every moment of our days, every penny of our money and every opportunity that is set before us, in the very best way that we can, so that nothing is wasted. Amen.

Tuesday:

Reading: John 6: 13–15.

Thought: Do we refuse honours?

Prayer: Grant that we may labour willingly without asking for any reward except that of knowing that we do Thy will. Amen.

Wednesday:

Reading: John 6: 16–21.

Thought: The presence of Jesus calms all storms.

Prayer: Dear Lord, when we are frightened by anything in life remind us of Your presence with us every minute of our lives. Amen.

Thursday:

Reading: John 6: 22–26.

Thought: What are our reasons for following Jesus?

Prayer: Lord Jesus, we want to be Your followers because we love You and know that You love us, and because we know that the way that You will lead us in will be the best way. Amen.

Friday:

Reading: John 6: 27–29.

Thought: Works cannot replace faith.

Prayer: Dear Lord, we know that the greatest thing that we can do to please You is to trust in You at all times and in all circumstances. Help us to do this, we pray You. Amen.

Saturday:

Reading: John 6: 30–35.

Thought: Have we accepted the bread of life?

Prayer: Gracious Lord, as we eat bread so that our bodies may grow, so feed us with the truths of Your Holy Word so that our hunger for goodness may be satisfied. Amen.

Sunday:

Reading: John 6: 66–69.

Thought: Are we convinced that Jesus is the Holy One of God?

Prayer: Lord Jesus, grant that throughout our lives we may never want to leave You, for we believe that You are the Holy One of God. Amen.

Grace for the Week:

We thank You, loving Lord,
For gifts of food and drink,
Be close beside us all the day
In everything we do and say
And everything we think.
Amen.

Monday:

Reading: Ecclesiastes 7: 8–10.

Thought: Do we finish what we start?

Prayer: Teach us to persevere, O God, and to finish those things that we start, and especially help us to persevere in the Christian life. Amen.

Tuesday:

Reading: Ecclesiastes 8: 11–13.

Thought: It will not be well with the wicked.

Prayer: Dear Father God, give us a godly fear of wrongdoing and a true longing to walk in Your ways. Amen.

Wednesday

Reading: 1 Samuel 1: 1, 2, 6, and 7.

Thought: Does our unkindness cause others to weep?

Prayer: Guard our tongues today, dear Lord, so that nothing we say may cause others to weep. Amen.

Thursday:

Reading: 1 Samuel 1: 8–10.

Thought: Do we take our troubles to the Lord?

Prayer: Teach us, dear Lord, to bring all our troubles to You when the actions of others fill our hearts with sadness. Amen.

Friday:

Reading: 1 Samuel 1: 11

Thought: Are our children given to the Lord?

Prayer: Dear Lord, we give ourselves again to You today and ask You to use each one of us in Your service. Amen.

Saturday:

Reading: 1 Samuel 1: 12–15.

Thought: Do we misjudge the actions of others?

Prayer: Forgive us, Lord, when we misjudge the actions of others and remind us that we are not able to know their inmost thoughts. Amen.

Sunday:

Reading: 1 Samuel 1: 16–18.

Thought: God does answer prayer.

Prayer: Dear God, we think especially today of those whose hearts are full of sorrow and pain. Answer their prayers, we beseech you, O Lord. Amen.

Grace for the Week:

Heavenly Father, we thank Thee for this food which Thou hast provided for us. In these days when famine stalks the earth teach us to share wisely and lovingly with Thy children in need. Amen.

Monday:

Reading: 1 Samuel 1: 19–20.

Thought: How do we start the day?

Prayer: Teach us to start the day with worship, dear Lord, so that we may have Your guidance for the hours that lie ahead. Amen.

Tuesday:

Reading: 1 Samuel 1: 21–23.

Thought: Promises should be kept.

Prayer: Help us to think carefully before we make a promise, because Your Word teaches us clearly that promises, once made, should never be broken. Amen.

Wednesday:

Reading: 1 Samuel 1: 24–28.

Thought: No one is too young to be taken to God's House.

Prayer: You have reminded us today, O Lord, that no one is too young to be taken to Your House or to be used in Your Service. Bless us as we worship together and try to serve You. Amen.

Thursday:

Reading: 1 Samuel 2: 1–2.

Thought: Are we glad in giving?

Prayer: When we make sacrifices for You, dear Lord Jesus, help us to do so gladly, and with joy. Amen.

Friday:

Reading: 1 Samuel 2: 18–21.

Thought: Sacrifice never goes unrewarded.

Prayer: Remind us, dear Lord, that You always reward us in Your own way and in Your own time, for any sacrifices that we make for You. Amen.

Saturday:

Reading: 1 Samuel 3: 1–5.

Thought: Do we take Your open Word for granted?

Prayer: Thank You for making Your Word open today to each one of us who will listen and obey. Amen.

Sunday:

Reading: 1 Samuel 3: 6–8.

Thought: Have we learned to recognize God's voice?

Prayer: Teach us to recognize Your voice when You speak to us alone in the quietness, dear Lord. Amen.

Grace for the Week:

We thank Thee now, dear Lord,
For homes and friends and food.
Grant us to serve Thee so this day
That we may show our gratitude.
Amen.

Monday:

Reading: 1 Samuel 3: 9 and 10.

Thought: Do we listen to the advice of older and wiser Christians?

Prayer: We thank You today, Lord, for those of our Christian friends who are older and wiser than we are. Help us to listen to their advice when we are in doubt. Amen.

Tuesday:

Reading: 1 Samuel 3: 11–13.

Thought: Have we control over our children?

Prayer: We pray today, Lord, that You will help us to have godly control over our children so that they may grow in love and knowledge of You. Amen.

Wednesday:

Reading: 1 Samuel 3: 15–17.

Thought: Does fear seal our lips?

Prayer: Make us brave to do the right and ready to speak the truth at all times, we beseech You, O Lord. Amen.

Thursday:

Reading: 1 Samuel 3: 18–20.

Thought: Do we bow to God's discipline?

Prayer: Give us a humble spirit, O Lord, that is content to accept at Your hand whatever seems good to You. Amen.

Friday:

Reading: 1 Samuel 8: 1–3.

Thought: Are we moved by the love of money?

Prayer: Dear Father God, help us always to overcome the temptation to do what is wrong for the hope of gaining money by our actions. Amen.

Saturday:

Reading: 1 Samuel 8: 4–6.

Thought: Are we afraid of being different?

Prayer: Dear Lord Jesus, we know that Your people have different loyalties and different standards from the rest of the world. Make us proud of our differences and not ashamed of them. Amen.

Sunday:

Reading: 1 Samuel 8: 7–10.

Thought: Do we want the Lord for our King?

Prayer: We remember today, dear God, that You are our Heavenly King. Make us loyal and brave subjects, we pray You. Amen.

Grace for the Week:

Our Father, as we gather about this table to share the food prepared and set before us, we thank You for all Your goodness and mercy towards us. Amen.

Monday:

Reading: 1 Samuel 8: 19–22.

Thought: Do we think we know better than God?

Prayer: Dear Lord Jesus, forgive us for the times when we pay no attention to Your voice and go our own wilful way. Help us to see that Your way is always the best. Amen.

Tuesday:

Reading: 1 Samuel 9: 1, 2 and 17.

Thought: Are we the right person for the job?

Prayer: Dear Heavenly Father, when someone is wanted to do a special job, show us clearly if we are the right person for it, and make us ready and willing to do our part. Amen.

Wednesday:

Reading: 1 Samuel 9: 22–24.

Thought: Do we give the best to others?

Prayer: Give us generous spirits, dear God, that make us eager to give the best that we have for the comfort of others. Amen.

Thursday:

Reading: 1 Samuel 10: 9–11.

Thought: Has God's Spirit changed us?

Prayer: Change our stubborn and selfish natures into the likeness of Yourself, O Loving Lord, so that others may see Your Spirit working within us. Amen.

Friday:

Reading: 1 Samuel 10: 17–19.

Thought: Have we turned away from God?

Prayer: We confess, dear Father, that sometimes we turn away from You and try to live our own lives. Remind us today that You are our Saviour and Lord. Amen.

Saturday:

Reading: 1 Samuel 10: 24–27.

Thought: Do we hold our peace?

Prayer: Dear Lord, when we know people are saying unkind things about us and thinking unkind thoughts about us, give us the wisdom to hold our peace. Amen.

Sunday:

Reading: 1 Samuel 11: 15; 12: 4.

Thought: Is our reputation blameless?

Prayer: Heavenly Father, please help us to live our lives cleanly and honestly, so that we may be found blameless in the Day of Judgment. Amen.

Grace for the Week:

Our Heavenly Father, we ask You to bless this food and our fellowship, and enable us to rejoice in the presence of the divine Unseen Guest, whose coming to earth has filled all life with new meaning and beauty. Amen.

Monday:

Reading: Philippians 4: 1–5.

Thought: Do we make up our differences?

Prayer: Gracious Lord, give us the spirit of forgiveness so that we may not hinder Your work by differences amongst us. Amen.

Tuesday:

Reading: Philippians 4: 6–7.

Thought: Don't worry.

Prayer: Teach us, dear Lord, to tell You every detail of our needs, and give us Your peace within our hearts. Amen.

Wednesday:

Reading: Philippians 4: 8–9.

Thought: What kind of things do we think about?

Prayer: Dear Father God, help us to think about the things that are true and honourable and pure and just and lovely and praiseworthy, for the sake of Him who was all these things. Amen.

Thursday:

Reading: Philippians 4: 10–12.

Thought: Content—whatever the circumstances.

Prayer: Teach us, Lord, to be content both when things are difficult and when things are easy, and help us always to be aware of the needs of those less fortunate than ourselves. Amen.

Friday:

Reading: Philippians 4: 13–17.

Thought: I can do all things in Him.

Prayer: When we are tempted to do wrong, dear God, remind us of Your power within us which can enable us to overcome any temptation or difficulty we may meet today. Amen.

Saturday:

Reading: Philippians 4: 18–20.

Thought: Is our generosity a "lovely fragrance"?

Prayer: Teach us the joy of giving willingly and generously to Your work, dear Lord, and show us where our gifts are most needed. Amen.

Sunday:

Reading: Psalm 127: 1–5.

Thought: Children are God's gift.

Prayer: We thank You, dear Lord, for the gift of children and the happiness they bring. Grant that each one may love and serve You throughout their lives. Amen.

SPECIAL WEEKS

Grace for the Week:

For every cup and plateful
God make us truly grateful. Amen.

Monday:

Reading: Matthew 26: 1–5.

Thought: Are we prepared to use tricks to get our own way?

Prayer: Dear Lord, forgive us for the times when we are prepared to act dishonestly in order to get our own way, and make us honest and upright in all our dealings. Amen.

Tuesday:

Reading: Matthew 26: 6–9.

Thought: Do we judge unkindly the actions of others?

Prayer: O Lord, we confess we are often guilty of criticizing and judging the actions of others. Give us more love and understanding for those who serve You in the way they think best. Amen.

Wednesday:

Reading: Matthew 26: 10–13.

Thought: Do we do "beautiful things" for Jesus?

Prayer: Dear Father God, give us a true longing to give You the very best of what we have and the very best of what we are. For the Lord Jesus Christ's sake. Amen.

Thursday:

Reading: Matthew 26: 14–16.

Thought: Is our loyalty for sale?

Prayer: Be very near us, dear Lord, at times when we are tempted to put aside our faith in You in the hope of worldly gain. Help us to stand firmly in Your strength. Amen.

Friday:

Reading: Matthew 26: 17–19.

Thought: Do we do what Jesus instructs us?

Prayer: Dear Lord, make us quick and willing to perform our ordinary, daily tasks, even if they are dull and uninteresting, remembering the readiness of Your disciples to obey your instructions. Amen.

Saturday:

Reading: Matthew 26: 20–23 and 25.

Thought: Does Jesus have a place at our meal table?

Prayer: Lord Jesus, be our Guest at this meal, we pray You, and may all we say and do be pleasing to You. Amen.

Sunday:

Reading: Matthew 26: 26–28.

Thought: Have we been freed from our sins?

Prayer: Cleanse us from our sin, Lord.

Make us clean within, Lord.

Make our hearts Your palace and Your royal throne. Amen.

Grace for the Week:

Dear Father, Your blessings to us are continuous. May we never grow weary in our thanksgiving to You for them. Accept the gratitude of our hearts for this food now before us, and for all other mercies with which our lives are daily blessed. Amen.

Monday:

Reading: Matthew 26: 31–35.

Thought: Do we ever lose faith?

Prayer: Loving Lord, You know that there are times when the faith of Your followers is sorely tried. Be with all those who face dangers and difficulties in Your Name today, and confirm their trust in You. Amen.

Tuesday:

Reading: Matthew 26: 36–39.

Thought: Not what I want but what God wants.

Prayer: Dear God, help us to pray sincerely today the prayer of the Lord Jesus, "Not what I want but what You want."

Amen.

Wednesday:

Reading: Matthew 26: 40–43.

Thought: Are we aware of our weaknesses?

Prayer: O Lord, we confess that sleepiness and sloth often prevent us from being in close and regular touch with You. Help us to be aware of this weakness and to overcome it. Amen.

Thursday:

Reading: Matthew 26: 44–46.

Thought: Do we take our ease when Jesus needs us?

Prayer: Dear Father in Heaven, often we fail to comfort and help our Christian brothers and sisters because we are unaware of their needs. Please keep us alert and watchful in Your service. Amen.

Friday:

Reading: Matthew 26: 47–50.

Thought: Do we betray our best friends?

Prayer: We thank you today, O Lord, for our friends. Remind us of the affection and loyalty we owe to them and may we never let them down or betray them by thought, word or deed. Amen.

Saturday:

Reading: Matthew 26: 51–54.

Thought: We cannot serve Jesus by blows.

Prayer: Lord Jesus, You know how often we are tempted to hit back at people in word and deed. Remind us that Your Kingdom cannot be served in this way. Amen.

Sunday:

Reading: Matthew 26: 55–58.

Thought: Do we follow Jesus at a safe distance?

Prayer: Dear Lord, help us to follow You fearlessly wherever You may lead, and forgive us for the times when we only follow at a "safe" distance. Amen.

Grace for the Week:

We thank Thee, Lord, for happy hearts,
For rain and sunny weather.
We thank Thee, Lord, for this our food,
And that we are together. Amen.

Monday:

Reading: Matthew 26: 59–63.

Thought: Do we know when to keep silent?

Prayer: Dear Lord, remind us today that sometimes we serve Your purposes better by our silence than our speech. Help us to discipline our tongues in Your service. Amen.

Tuesday:

Reading: Matthew 26: 64–68.

Thought: We shouldn't be bullied into lying.

Prayer: Dear Lord, You know that there are times when we are tempted to tell or act a lie because we are afraid to tell the truth. Give us a special measure of Your courage and strength so that we take our stand for truth and honesty. Amen.

Wednesday:

Reading: Matthew 26: 69–72.

Thought: Do we conceal our relationship with Jesus?

Prayer: Lord Jesus, we confess with shame that we are not always ready and willing to confess that we are Your disciples amongst those who do not know or serve You. Please make us more ready to witness for You at all times. Amen.

Thursday:

Reading: Matthew 26: 73–75.

Thought: "Peter remembered the saying of Jesus."

Prayer: Dear Father God. write all Your words upon our hearts and imprint them in our memories so that they may come back to us when we need your correction or guidance. Amen.

Friday:

Reading: Matthew 27: 3–5.

Thought: It is sometimes too late to make amends.

Prayer: O Lord, we remember today that some wrongs can be righted by apologies and some by deeds, but some can never be righted at all. Forgive us for all our wrongdoing and make us more watchful and thoughtful and wary in the future. Amen.

Saturday:

Reading: Matthew 27: 11–14.

Thought: Jesus was slow to defend Himself.

Prayer: Dear Father God, we confess how quickly we jump to our own defence. Give us Your peace of mind so that we do not mind what other people say about us as long as our hearts are right with You. Amen.

Sunday:

Reading: Matthew 27: 15–19.

Thought: Do we make the right choice?

Prayer: Almighty God, we bring before You today the choices that we will have to make, as yet unknown to us but known to You. Give us wisdom to choose rightly, we pray You. Amen.

Grace for the Week:

Our Heavenly Father, You make the sun to shine on the just and the unjust. You give food to the thankful and the unthankful. We would be numbered among those who give You thanks for all Your blessings. In Jesus' Name. Amen.

Monday:

Reading: Matthew 27: 20–23.

Thought: What shall I do with Jesus?

Prayer: We pray today, Lord, for those who will be making a choice between following You and following their own way. Give them the wisdom to choose rightly. Amen.

Tuesday:

Reading: Matthew 27: 24–26.

Thought: We cannot shirk responsibility.

Prayer: We bring before You today, Lord, those in high positions who must make important and binding decisions. Give them courage and honesty to decide wisely. Amen.

Wednesday:

Reading: Matthew 27: 27–29.

Thought: Do we bow low in sincerity or mockery?

Prayer: We confess, dear God, how easy it is to bow our heads to You without real thought or meaning, but as we wait before You in the quietness now we would worship You with true respect. Amen.

Thursday:

Reading: Matthew 27: 30–32.

Thought: Are we reluctant to carry the Cross?

Prayer: Dear Father, make us more willing to shoulder the burdens that following You may put upon us, so that our service is not forced or grudgingly given. Amen.

Good Friday:

Reading: Matthew 27: 33–37.

Thought: Is Jesus our King?

Prayer: You died today, gracious Lord, so that You might be King, not of the Jews only but of all those who love You. We thank You for dying for us, that through You our sins could be forgiven. Amen.

Saturday:

Reading: Matthew 28: 1–6.

Thought: He has risen, as He said.

Prayer: We thank you today, Lord, because we know we can have such perfect trust in your words. Remind us of this when we are tempted to doubt the truth of anything that You have said. Amen.

Easter Sunday:

Reading: Matthew 28: 7–10.

Thought: Hearts filled with great joy.

Prayer: Our hearts are filled with great joy and thankfulness for the hope and wonder of the Easter message today, Lord, and we praise You for the wonderful gift of everlasting life. Amen.

Grace for the Week:

The Lord our pastures shall prepare, and feed us with a shepherd's care. His presence shall our wants supply, and guard us with a watchful eye. Amen.

Monday:

Reading: Matthew 28: 11–15.

Thought: Can people buy our silence?

Prayer: We ask for Your courage to speak the truth at all times, Lord, and grant that we may never be guilty of hiding the truth with lies. Amen.

Tuesday:

Reading: Matthew 28: 16–20

Thought: "Some doubted."

Prayer: We claim Your promise today, Lord, that You will be with us always. Make us specially conscious of Your presence in times of doubt and difficulty, we pray You. Amen.

Wednesday:

Reading: Philippians 2: 1–3.

Thought: Being of the same mind.

Prayer: Dear Lord, help us to live together in harmony and love, being of the same mind and thinking more of each other than we do of ourselves. Amen.

Thursday:

Reading: Philippians 2: 4–5.

Thought: Do we see things from other people's point of view?

Prayer: Dear Father, we confess to You now how often we think only of our own affairs. Teach us to consider the other person's point of view. Amen.

Friday:

Reading: Philippians 2: 12–13.

Thought: God is at work within us.

Prayer: Dear Lord Jesus, work within our stubborn hearts, we pray You, giving us the will and the power to achieve Your purpose. Amen.

Saturday:

Reading: Philippians 2: 14–16.

Thought: Do we do our work without grumbling or arguing?

Prayer: Heavenly Father, we ask Your forgiveness for the times when we grumble and argue about what we have to do. Help us to be more cheerful and willing. Amen.

Sunday:

Reading: Philippians 2: 19–22.

Thought: Do we look after our own interests?

Prayer: Give us, dear Lord, a true concern for Your business upon earth and a real interest in the well-being of other Christians. Amen.

Whit Sunday

Reading: Acts 2: 1–4.

Thought: Does our power come from the Holy Spirit?

Prayer: We pray today, Lord, not for earthly power, but for the power of Your Holy Spirit upon us, so that we may be equipped to do Your will. Amen.

Grace for the Week:

Our Father, we give Thee grateful thanks for this food. Bless it to the nourishment of our bodies; bless our home; keep us and our loved ones, through Jesus Christ our Lord. Amen.

Monday:

Reading: Mark 1: 1–4.

Thought: Are we helping to make paths straight?

Prayer: Take away the crookedness from our paths so that our life's walk may be a straight one. Amen.

Tuesday:

Reading: Mark 1: 5–8.

Thought: We must always look forward to something better.

Prayer: Dear Lord, help us not to become satisfied with our own present efforts, but always to look forward and press onwards. Amen.

Wednesday:

Reading: Mark 1: 9–11.

Thought: Is God pleased with us?

Prayer: Dear Father God, we confess how seldom our thoughts and words and deeds are pleasing to You. Forgive us and help us to do better in the future. Amen.

Thursday:

Reading: Mark 1: 12–15.

Thought: Testing comes before preaching.

Prayer: O Lord, help us to stand firm when we are tested so that we may be fit people to preach the good news of God. Amen.

Friday:

Reading: Mark 1: 16–18.

Thought: Are we fishers of men?

Prayer: Teach us to follow closely in Your footsteps, Lord Jesus, so that we too may become fishers of men. Amen.

Saturday:

Reading: Mark 1: 19–22.

Thought: Do we recognize the authority of Jesus?

Prayer: Teach us from Your Word, O Lord, and fill us with wonder at Your sayings. Amen.

Sunday:

Reading: Mark 1: 23–27.

Thought: Are we less obedient than the unclean spirits?

Prayer: Dear Lord Jesus, even the unclean spirits recognized Your voice and obeyed it. Teach us to do likewise, we pray You. Amen.

Grace for the Week:

We fold our hands and softly say,
Thank You, Lord, for our food today.
Amen.

Monday:

Reading: Mark 1: 28–31.

Thought: Do we take care of the needs of others?

Prayer: Dear Father God, thank you for the gift of good health. Remind us to use our energies in caring for the needs of others. Amen.

Tuesday:

Reading: Mark 1: 32–35.

Thought: Do we refresh ourselves with prayer?

Prayer: Holy Spirit of God, when we become weary and overworked, teach us to find a quiet place and give ourselves up to prayer so that our spirits may be encouraged and refreshed. Amen.

Wednesday:

Reading: Mark 1: 36–39.

Thought: Have we a purpose in life?

Prayer: Dear Lord Jesus, help us to see clearly our purpose in life and show us how we may fulfil it. Amen.

Thursday:

Reading: Mark 1: 40–42.

Thought: Do we make our requests on our knees?

Prayer: Teach us, dear Lord, to make our requests on our knees, and give us the faith to believe that You can grant them. Amen.

Friday:

Reading: Mark 1: 43–45.

Thought: Does our disobedience hinder God's plans?

Prayer: Forgive us, Lord, for the many times when our direct disobedience hinders the working of Your plans. Amen.

Saturday:

Reading: Isaiah 7: 14 and 15.

Thought: Do we recognize God's "signs"?

Prayer: Help us, dear God, to be ever watchful so that we may recognize Your hand at work in the world today. Amen.

Sunday:

Reading: Isaiah 61: 1 and 2.

Thought: Are we God's messengers?

Prayer: Use us as Your messengers, dear Lord, to tell Your Good News to those with whom we come in contact. Amen.

Grace for the week:

Jesus, born of Mary, in a stable bleak and bare,
We bow our heads and thank you now
For special Christmas fare. Amen.

Monday:

Reading: Micah 5: 2–4.

Thought: Great things spring from humble beginnings.

Prayer: O Lord God, who planned that the Lord Jesus should be born of humble parents in a lowly home, use what we are and what we have in your service. Amen.

Tuesday:

Reading: Zechariah 9: 9–10.

Thought: Do our words command peace?

Prayer: Dear Father God, as we think of the One whose message was peace and goodwill, take control of our lives and tongues this Christmastide so that we may be like Him. Amen.

Wednesday:

Reading: Malachi 3: 1–2.

Thought: Are we ready for the Lord?

Prayer: As we prepare for Christmas and the celebration of Your birth, search our hearts, dear Lord, and show us if there is anything displeasing to you. Amen.

Thursday:

Reading: Matthew 1: 18–21.

Thought: Do we obey God or our own feelings?

Prayer: Dear God, You know there are times when what we want to do does not agree with Your will. Speak to us and give us obedient hearts. Amen.

Friday:

Reading: Matthew 1: 22–25.

Thought: Is God with us?

Prayer: Dear God, please live within our home and inside each one of us both today and in the future, as you have promised in Your Holy Word. Amen.

Saturday:

Reading: Matthew 2: 1–3.

Thought: The Wise Men searched.

Prayer: Give us the desire, O God, to search until we find, to ask until we receive, and to knock until the door of everlasting life is opened to us. Amen.

Sunday:

Reading: Matthew 2: 4–7.

Thought: Do we know what is contained in God's writings?

Prayer: Give us a renewed hunger to read and understand Your Holy Word, so that we may be led to search out the truths that it contains. Amen.

Grace for the Week:

Our Father, You are the Giver of all good gifts. Teach us to accept what You give us with thanksgiving and with the desire to use all for You. Amen.

Monday:

Reading: Matthew 2: 8–11.

Thought: A meeting with Jesus always brings joy.

Prayer: Dear Lord Jesus, we cannot give You costly gifts, but what we have we offer to You with loving and grateful hearts. Amen.

Tuesday:

Reading: Matthew 2: 12–15.

Thought: Do we obey promptly?

Prayer: Speak clearly to us we beseech You, O Lord, when it is in Your will that we go or stay, and make us prompt in our obedience. Amen.

Wednesday:

Reading: Mark 2: 1–2.

Thought: Do we keep open house for those who need Jesus?

Prayer: Heavenly Father, use our home for Your work so that others may learn about You. Amen.

Thursday:

Reading: Mark 2: 3–5.

Thought: Are we prepared to overcome difficulties to bring our friends to Jesus?

Prayer: Dear Lord Jesus, give us such a real concern for our friends that we are prepared to overcome great difficulties in order to bring them face to face with You. Amen.

Friday:

Reading: Mark 2: 6–11.

Thought: Jesus has knowledge of all our thoughts.

Prayer: Remind us, dear Lord, that You know all our secret thoughts and that nothing is hidden from You. Amen.

Saturday:

Reading: Mark 2: 12.

Thought: Do we give glory to God for His wonderful works?

Prayer: O Lord God, we are full of wonder as we see all Your marvellous works, and we give You the glory for all that You have done. Amen.

Sunday:

Reading: Mark 2: 13–14.

Thought: Do we listen to, and answer, God's call?

Prayer: Heavenly Father, help us to listen to Your word and obey Your voice when you speak to us. Amen.